W9-AJT-083

# READ ABOUT THE
# POSTMAN

# READ ABOUT THE
# POSTMAN

*written and illustrated by*

Louis Slobodkin

FRANKLIN WATTS, INC.
575 Lexington Avenue
New York, N.Y. 10022

Library of Congress Catalog Card Number: 66-12143
Copyright © 1966 by Louis Slobodkin
Printed in the United States of America
1  2  3  4  5

## Your Friend, the Postman

Do you know that there are over 200 million pieces of mail — letters, parcels, magazines, news-papers, advertisements, and other such things — sent and delivered in the United States every day? And when you think that just one piece in that daily 200 million may be a letter for you from your friend in faraway Timbuctoo — or right around the corner in your own town — and that letter is delivered right to your door, you realize that the postman is a wonderful person.

That is true of postmen all over the United States, and the rest of the world too.

All your friend had to do to send that letter was to write the proper address, and paste the proper stamp on the envelope. Then in a day or two that letter was delivered to you, perhaps thousands of miles away.

But sending and receiving messages, letters, and packages was not always so easy nor were they delivered so fast.

AN ANCIENT PERSIAN POST CARD ⟶

THE LETTERING IS CALLED CUNEIFORM

IN ENGLISH IT SAYS

"HAVING WONDERFUL TIME. WISH YOU WERE HERE."

## The First Clay Postcards

It is said that about 4,400 years ago the first written message that was ever sent from one person to another was delivered in ancient Persia.

This is the story.

The king of that land had a number of slaves who carried his messages to all parts of his kingdom.

The king once said to his most trusted slave, "Keep a wise head upon thy shoulders and thy tongue between thy teeth."

That was very good advice, and it was especially good for that slave and the other slave messengers because in those days they carried their messages in their heads.

The king did not write down his message. The messenger had to memorize it.

The king's most trusted slave often took along the king's ring to prove that the important message he carried was really from the king.

Then one day the slave had a very good idea. He was afraid that he might lose the ring or that it might be stolen, so he suggested that the king keep his own ring and press it down into a flat piece of clay. The clay was dried in the sun until it was hard, and then the slave carried the impression of the king's ring instead of the ring itself. All the other slave messengers were also given pieces of clay showing the impression of the king's ring, to prove that their messages really came from the king.

Later on, the king's messages were written or cut into the flat pieces of clay, and the king's ring was pressed into the clay. Finally, the pieces of clay were sun-dried and carried away by the messengers. Those messages cut into clay and signed with the impression of the king's ring were the first postcards that were sent and delivered.

# The First Secret Letter

Over three thousand years ago an Egyptian king named Amenhotep IV sent a very important secret message with his servant.

This is how the message was kept secret. The king ordered all the hair shaved from the servant's head. Then he wrote his message on the bare skin of the servant's skull. The servant was kept alone for a month until his hair grew back again. No one saw him or spoke to him during that time. His food and drink were passed through a small hole in the door of the cell where he lived.

When he was finally released he carried his secret message to the place where the king sent him. No one along the way knew where the mes-

sage was hidden. When the messenger got to the proper person, his head was shaved again and the king's message was read. Of course, the servant did not wash his head for months during that period.

Nowadays there is a much more hygienic and quicker way to get a private or secret message from one person to another. Just write your letter, put it in an envelope, seal the flap down, and stick a first-class stamp on the envelope.

Nobody anywhere, no matter who he is, is allowed to open that letter except the person to whom you sent it. In this country, only the United States postal inspectors may open other people's mail. And they may do this only when they have good reason to believe that the mail contains something dangerous, or when they have some other very important official reason.

Your letter with a first-class stamp on it may travel over a thousand miles in one day. It took the Egyptian servant a couple of months to deliver the king's message to a place only three hundred miles away. He carried the message from the city of Thebes, where the king lived, to the city of Memphis, where the letter was delivered.

10

# The Greek and Roman Messengers

In 490 B.C. another very important message was carried by the fastest Greek runner of that time. He ran twenty-six miles as fast as he could go, from the Battle of Marathon, to tell the news of the battle to the people of the great Greek city of Athens. He could only gasp, "Victory is ours! Athens is saved!" as he ran into the marketplace. Then he fell down, dead.

The great marathon race that is run by the famous athletes from all over the world who meet at the Olympic Games is held in honor of that brave runner who gave his life to "carry the mail" to Athens.

NEITHER SNOW NOR RAIN NOR HEAT NOR GLOOM OF NIGHT STAYS THESE COURIERS FROM THE SWIFT COMPLETION OF THEIR APPOINTED ROUNDS.

These fine words are carved into the walls of many post offices all over the United States. They were written by Herodotus, who was one of the world's first historians. He wrote these words about the great messengers and mail carriers of the ancient days.

A few hundred years later, the postmen of Rome traveled on foot, on horseback, and by chariots on the excellent roads that the Romans had built throughout Europe, from Rome way up to Scotland. Stone posts marked each mile of these roads, and there were stations where sometimes as many as forty horses were kept for the postmen so that they could rest and get fresh mounts.

The word "post" comes from a Latin word for a "station" or "place." (Latin was the language used by the ancient Romans.) "Post," "postal," "postman," "post road," and all the similar words we use when we talk about the postal service come from that old Latin word, positus.

The messages that the Roman postmen carried
were usually from the emperor of Rome to his
generals all over Europe, or from the generals to
the emperor. These important secret messages
were written on hard wax tablets with a pointed
instrument about the size of a pencil. It was called
a stylus. If any of the enemies of Rome caught
one of the emperor's postmen, the postman quickly
wiped over the wax and destroyed the message.

Some of the old Roman post roads are still used
in Europe. Along them the Roman postmen traveled as much as 165 miles a day.

## The Royal Postal Service

Over the years, many private messenger services were started. About five hundred years ago an Italian family called Tassi began a regular postal service that served Germany, Austria, Italy, and Spain. The Tassis' postal service carried messages from one king or nobleman to another. Their messengers also carried presents of jewels and other valuable treasures from one country to another. They fought off bandits who tried to steal the messages and the gifts. The Tassi family ran their postal service for over three hundred years. In time, they became nobles and some of them changed their names to De la Tour et Tassis.

14

## A Postal Service for Everyone

In about 1400, the common people also began to send messages and letters to one another. In 1461, Louis XI, King of France, set up the first real postal system that served all the people of France. This postal service was too expensive for the average Frenchman. But now anyone who could afford to pay could send a letter to a distant friend.

Not many persons could write, but there were letter writers who for a few small coins would take down a letter. And since not everyone could read, the local priest or someone else would read the letter to the person who received it.

These letters were often sent with the merchants and priests who traveled throughout the land.

# The Butcher Postal Service

The men who carried most of the letters for the common people of Holland, Belgium, and Germany were the traveling butchers. In those days, butchers journeyed from one farm to the next to slaughter the pigs, sheep, and cattle for the farmers, and they also went to cattle fairs and cattle markets. As they traveled, they carried letters from one friend to another.

There was a regular butcher postal service, and the rulers of the various countries gave the messengers protection just as if they were government mail carriers.

# La Petite Post

The first city mail delivery service is said to have been started in Paris, France, on August 8, 1653. A man called De Velayer was allowed by the King of France to start this regular postal service.

De Velayer placed boxes all over Paris to receive letters, and he put up signs asking the Parisians to use his postal service. The signs explained how good the service was for people who had no servants to carry messages, and for shopkeepers who did not want to leave their shops to deliver bills. The boxes were emptied three times a day, at 6 A.M., at 11 A.M., and at 3 P.M. Then the mail was sorted and delivered.

De Velayer sold pieces of paper to be wrapped around the letters or packages that people wanted to mail. The wrappers cost just two sous. A sou is a French coin much smaller than a penny and of much less value. The money that De Velayer received paid him for his work.

At first the people of Paris laughed at De Velayer's postal business or, as it was called, La Petite Poste. They used it for sending funny letters and invitations to each other. But they soon forgot about the service, and De Velayer went out of business.

A hundred years later, in 1758, another Frenchman, Claude de Chamousset, again started a postal service in Paris. He made so much money by it that the government officials took his business away from him and ran the city postal service themselves.

## The First Postmaster

Regular postal service started in England about the time of King Henry VIII. Around 1533, he appointed a man called Sir Brian Tuke as Master of the Post, and asked him to set up a good postal system. But it was not until Henry VIII's daughter, Queen Elizabeth, came to the throne of England that a whole postal system was set up.

Messengers on horseback delivered the mail. Every time the queen traveled, a new post office was started so that she could receive her letters. Soon there were post offices all over England. In

the beginning these post offices were for the queen and the nobility only. But as the common people learned to read and write they too used the postal service.

## The First Postmarks

The first postmarks on a letter to show what post office the letter came from and what day it was mailed were used in England about 1660. Henry Bishop was postmaster general of England at that time. In those days, postmasters general paid for the right to run the postal service. They did not work for the government as they do now.

Mr. Bishop ordered the postal carriers who worked for him to mark each letter as it came into one of his post offices so that it showed the day of the month it was received. He wanted the letters delivered promptly and did not want old ones cluttering up his post offices. After all, he was in the post-office business to make money, not to store old letters. Postmarks were then called "Bishop's marks."

For the next two hundred years the postboy with his post horn and with his leather mail pouches slung across the saddle was a familiar sight on the roads of England. It was the rule that he must blow his post horn four times in every mile, so that people with letters to send would know he was coming. Another rule was that he must ride at the rate of seven miles an hour in summer and five miles an hour in winter.

But the postal service was slow and uncertain. The postboys were often attacked by robbers, and the mailbags were stolen. The postboys often dawdled along the way.

Sometimes the people who sent letters wrote on the envelope, "Haste, post, haste for thy life, for thy life, haste," to spur the postboys on. Other people drew a skull and crossbones alongside the address on the envelope to scare the postboy into doing his duty quickly.

# The Mail Coaches

From 1784 to 1830, mail coaches rattled swiftly along the roads of England. The guard sitting in back of the driver of the coach blew his horn as they approached a town, and the postmaster of the town would be ready to throw a mail sack onto the coach, or to receive a mail sack.

It is said that one night the sleepy wife of a postmaster opened her bedroom window and tossed to the roof of the mail coach what she thought was a mailbag. When morning came, she found she had thrown her husband's leather breeches onto the mail coach and still had the mailbag.

The mail coaches were much faster than the postboys. They went ten miles an hour — so fast that there was some talk of stopping them. At that time, people believed that traveling in the coaches at such a great speed would make a person sick.

But the mail coaches were not stopped until the railroads came along.

# The First American Post Office

In America, the first beginnings of a post office were set up in Boston in 1639, when the English ruled that city.

Before that, letters from England to America were given to the captains of ships sailing to the American colonies. Any sea captain going to the colonies let everyone in the English port from which he sailed know about it. A large bag was placed in one of the coffeehouses where people came to drink coffee or tea and eat meat pies and buttered scones. The people would put their letters in the big bag, and it was closed and taken aboard the ship the day she sailed for America.

This was not a very good scheme. No one took care of the letters to see that they were delivered to the right people. The whole bag was usually dumped onto the table of a seaport tavern when the ship arrived in America, and the letters lay there for months. Anybody who came along could handle them. By the time a person did get a letter addressed to him it was covered with dirty fingerprints and stained from spilled drinks. Most of

the letters were lost and never did get to the right people.

Then, in 1639, the General Court of Massachusetts ordered that all mail brought into Boston by ship, and all mail to be sent to England, must be delivered to Fairbanks Tavern. That tavern was on the Boston waterfront, and everyone knew the place. If someone expected mail from England, or if he wanted to send a letter there, he would go to Fairbanks Tavern.

Richard Fairbanks, the owner of the tavern, was in charge of the mail. He got one penny for every letter he handled, and he gave the incoming letters to the proper people in the colonies.

A little later, while the Dutch ruled New York, which was then called New Amsterdam, the Dutch government passed a law forbidding anyone to carry letters across the ocean unless he had an official right to do so. In the government offices in Holland the Dutch put up a box for people who wanted to send letters to New Amsterdam. They also put up a box in New Amsterdam for letters to be sent to Holland. The New Amsterdam government charged "three stivers in wampum" for each letter. A stiver is a small Dutch coin worth about two cents.

When the English took New Amsterdam away from the Dutch and named the city New York, they set up a regular postal service between New York and Boston. Men on horseback carried leather bags full of letters, and followed old Indian trails through the wilderness between the two towns.

Francis Lovelace, governor of the New York colony, sent the first letter to Boston on January 22, 1673. It took two weeks for the lonely mailman to reach Boston.

Governor Lovelace's mail service lasted less than seven months, because the Dutch sailed into New York Harbor and captured the city again. But about fifty years later, long after the English had chased the Dutch out of New York once more, a

regular mail service between New York and Boston was established on what is now known as the Boston Post Road.

The postriders who carried the mail earned extra money by doing errands for the settlers along the road. They sometimes had to fight off Indians as they rode through the wilderness. But at other times everything was very quiet and peaceful as they rode along. Some postriders whiled away the long, tiresome journey by knitting as they jogged along on their horses.

## Benjamin Franklin, Postmaster

In 1737, Benjamin Franklin became the deputy postmaster of Philadelphia, Pennsylvania. A few years later he became the deputy postmaster general of all the English colonies in America.

As deputy postmaster general, Benjamin Franklin ran all the post offices in the colonies so well that for the first time the American Post Office Department was able to earn money instead of losing it, and that money was sent to England.

In spite of that, Benjamin Franklin was dismissed in 1774 because he began to work and plan with many other great colonial Americans for a United States of America.

Benjamin Franklin was not out of the postmaster's job very long though, because the American Revolution began, and one of the first things the Continental Congress did was to set up a United States postal system with Benjamin Franklin in charge.

Certain important officials in the government were allowed to send their letters through the mails without stamps. This was called a franking (or free) privilege. On their letters the senders then signed their names as Mr. Franklin did — "Free, B. Franklin."

That is the way he wrote it when he worked for the English. But after the Declaration of Independence was signed and Mr. Franklin worked for the United States of America he signed his name, "B. Free Franklin."

# Mail By Steamship

The first steamship to cross the Atlantic Ocean from America to Europe sailed on May 24, 1819. The ship left from Savannah, Georgia, and was called the "Savannah." Even though there were cabins elegantly furnished in plush and gold, and though the shipowners did all they could to attract people to come aboard, no passengers sailed on that first trip. People were afraid the fire from the engines would set fire to the ship.

But the postmaster general of the United States

was not frightened. On the "Savannah" 's first trip he sent a man named Nathaniel Crane with a sack of mail for Europe. That was the first time any mail was delivered overseas by steamship anywhere in the world.

The ship carried sails as well as a steam engine, and as she crossed the ocean she sailed most of the time, when the wind was right. In the twenty-seven days of the Atlantic crossing she steamed along for only about eight hours. Off the coast of Ireland a British ship came to help because the captain saw the "Savannah" 's smoke and thought the ship was afire.

# The Mail Trains

So far, mail had been carried by men on foot and on horseback, and by chariot, stagecoach, sailing ship, and steamship. Now, at last, mail was carried by railroad.

In America, in 1832, the Camden & Amboy Railroad of New Jersey and the Saratoga & Schenectady Railroad of New York began carrying the mail.

At first, when the trains went at twelve miles an hour, the Camden and Amboy charged the United States $100 a mile. Later, when the trains were able to go twenty miles an hour, the railroad com-

pany asked $300 a mile to carry the mail.

In those days, trains did not always run on time. There were many breakdowns, and passengers often had to get out and cut wood and carry water for the engines. Cattle often stopped the mail trains by standing on the tracks. The railroad trains only ran during daylight hours. If a train did not reach a town or city by sunset it stopped, wherever it was. Mail delivery was not as fast as it might have been.

A clerk who had charge of the mail on one of the trains had a good idea. He started to sort out the mail on the train between New York and Boston. When the train reached Boston, the mail was all ready to be delivered by the Boston postmen.

Ever since then, a great deal of the mail to the big cities has been sorted out on the moving trains.

In about 1865, after the Civil War, the railroad mail-carrying became even better. Special mail cars were built by the railroad companies all over the country. They were anxious to carry the mail because they found that the job paid them well.

Catcher arms of metal were put up on the mail cars so that mail clerks could pick up mailbags from stations even while the trains were traveling at a high speed. The iron horse, as the railroad engine was called in those days, became the fastest and best way of carrying the mail.

# Mail for the West

As the people of the United States began to go west to the new territories — some of them to dig for gold in California, others to start farming or raising cattle out on the prairie — they wanted mail delivered, too. No railroad tracks crossed the Great Plains to the West.

The United States Post Office Department was still growing, but not fast enough.

Some men started to carry mail for other people out in the wild West. In San Francisco one man, Alexander Todd, an ex-miner, charged one dollar to deliver a letter to the goldfields. Later on, he charged one ounce of gold dust, worth about fifteen dollars in those days. And he sold three-month-old New York newspapers for as much as eight dollars apiece to the gold miners in California.

Next, many private express companies began carrying mail out to the West. The most important was Wells Fargo & Company. This company bought stamped envelopes from the government for two cents apiece, then put its own stamp on the envelope and charged ten cents to deliver a letter.

Wells Fargo & Company had stagecoaches, wagons, and riders who raced across the plains, carrying the mail. Often the mail carriers had to fight off savage Indians and stagecoach robbers.

But even the express companies were not fast enough for the people out West who wanted to send and receive letters.

## The Pony Express

About that time three men named Russell, Majors, and Waddell, who were well known to everyone out West for their freighting business, laid plans for a speedier way of getting mail across the plains. They placed this advertisement in the newspapers.

They gathered the hardest-riding young men and the fastest horses they could find, and started to race the mail across the country to California from St. Joseph, Missouri, where the railroad tracks and the telegraph wires from the East Coast

37

ended. They raced through parts of Missouri, Kansas, Nebraska, Colorado, Wyoming, Utah, Nevada, and California, across the plains, the deserts, and the wilderness. This mail service was called the Pony Express.

Stations for the express were placed from ten to fifteen miles apart across the plains. Good, fast, fresh horses waited at each station, and there were food and places for the men and horses to sleep. Each station was guarded, to fight off Indians and outlaws.

The first trip of the Pony Express started on April 3, 1860. A special train had roared across the country from the East Coast, carrying the Pony

Express mail. At St. Jo, as St. Joseph was called, a fast rider grabbed the mail and raced his horse west to the first station out on the plains. There he jumped quickly from his horse, mounted a fresh horse, and raced on to the next station. And so it went. All the way across the plains, Pony Express riders hurried the mail to California. At the same time, mail from California was being rushed east.

Each horseman rode from 75 to 100 miles across the plains each day. At every station the riders changed their horses in just two minutes. They traveled by day and throughout the night. Robbers, bandits, and savage Indians tried to catch

them. Sometimes they did. Some Pony Express riders were wounded, some may have been killed, but most of the time the mail did get through.

The Pony Express riders became the heroes of the West. They wore broad-brimmed hats, buckskin shirts, cloth trousers, and high boots. The packs of letters they carried in their mail pouches were carefully wrapped in light oiled silk to protect them from the rain, and the sweat of the horses.

The mail each man carried weighed just twenty pounds. Only letters were taken. They were written on thin tissue paper. At first the Pony Express charged five dollars for every half-ounce of mail the riders carried. Two sheets of thin paper and an envelope weighed about half an ounce. Later the company charged only one dollar for a half-ounce of mail so that more people would send their letters by Pony Express.

One young Pony Express rider was named Will Cody. Later he became known as Buffalo Bill and was famous all over the world. He was only sixteen years old when he became a Pony Express rider.

In 1861, when Abraham Lincoln was inaugurated and made his first speech as President of the United States, the Pony Express riders carried copies of the speech from St. Jo to San Francisco, California, in seven days and seventeen hours. That is a distance of 1,950 miles.

There is a story about one of the young riders known as "Pony Bob" Haslam. He carried President Lincoln's speech from Smith's Creek and sped west to Fort Churchill. He was mounted on a horse called Old Buck when he met a band of unfriendly Indians. They were riding stolen Pony Express horses.

The Indians chased Pony Bob and Old Buck. Usually a Pony Express rider had no trouble getting away from Indians, because the Pony Express horses were much faster than the horses the Indians rode. But these Indians were mounted on good, fresh, swift Pony Express horses.

Although he hated to do it, young Pony Bob de-

cided that he had to shoot those fine Pony Express horses if he hoped to escape and save the mail. He did shoot the horses and fight off the Indians by firing revolvers with both hands, and the mail was carried through — but not before the Indians had shot an arrow into Pony Bob's left arm, and another arrow had torn into his cheek and knocked out five teeth.

When Pony Bob, riding Old Buck, reached the next station, where a fresh horse was waiting, he spent a few minutes caring for his wounds. Then he went on to finish his run to Fort Churchill, where another rider carried President Lincoln's speech farther west.

Many stories which may or may not have been true were told about the Pony Express. For example, it is said that the wives and sweethearts of the Pony Express riders used to bake cookies and cakes and have them ready when the men came dashing by. That may very well be true.

But this story is more doubtful. It has been said that the doughnut was invented by a sweetheart of one of the riders. The story is that she baked small cakes with holes in their centers so that her friend the Pony Express rider could catch them on the barrel of his rifle as he rode by.

When telegraph wires were stretched across the plains, and people were able to send telegrams, the Pony Express was finished. A year and a half after it started, the Pony Express was gone. But the brave and fearless riders and the stories of how they carried the mail will never be forgotten.

# Airmail Pigeon Post

One of the oldest ways of sending messages from one person to another is by pigeon post. Homing pigeons can be trained to fly with little tubes attached to their legs or tail feathers.

Messages written on rolled-up slips of very thin paper are slid into the tubes, and away go the pigeons.

A pigeon who lives in New York may be carried in a small coop to a place several hundred miles away — Buffalo, or Cincinnati, or even a more distant town. There a tiny letter is slipped into his tube, and back he streaks. He travels without a map and without a compass, but somehow he manages to fly to his home in New York again.

The ancient Chinese, Persians, Hebrews, and Greeks all sent messages by pigeon post, and for hundreds of years pigeons were used by armies all over the world.

Until very recently the United States Army had a regular Pigeon Corps. Some of the pigeons that were used to carry messages in World War I even walked back to their home coops when for some reason they could not fly. One brave pigeon who was wounded received a medal.

During one war in the past century the pigeon post was especially useful. That was in 1870 and 1871, when France and Germany were fighting. The German army surrounded the city of Paris, the capital of France.

No messages, mail, or news could get through the German lines. The telegraph wires that the French had hidden at the bottom of the Seine River, which flows through Paris, were cut by the Germans. The French filled light copper balls full of letters and floated them down the river at night, trying to get messages out of the city. But the Germans caught the copper balls in nets. Small balloons were sent up into the air with letters tied to them. Some balloons, pushed by the wind, passed over the German lines, but there was no sure way of getting news and letters in and out of Paris.

At last someone thought of pigeons!

Manned balloons were sent up to take the mail out of Paris. With every balloon there was a basket of homing pigeons.

M. Rampont, the postmaster general of all France, went up in a balloon at the French city of Tours. He had with him three pigeons who lived in Paris. Each of the pigeons carried a number of letters. When he released those pigeons they flew off, and two of them reached Paris, but the third

was never heard from again. From then on, the
pigeon post to Paris was established and it was
very successful.

When the German guns could not stop the pigeons, the German soldiers sent up hawks to at-
tack them. Some pigeons were caught, but the
pigeon post went on. If the French had tied whis-
tles and little bells to their pigeons, as the ancient
Chinese did, the hawks would have been frightened away and the lost pigeons would have been
saved.

The French wrote their letters on the very thin-
nest paper. Then they rolled up the letters and

slipped them into pieces of goose quill about two inches long. The goose quills were tied to the pigeons' tail feathers. But one pigeon could carry only two or three tiny letters, and the writing was so small it was hard to read, and even harder to put down in the first place.

The French tried many other ways of writing their letters, until they found that if they printed them, and photographed them very, very, very small on film, they could send 2,500 letters and dispatches on a tiny sheet of film.

These films were so small that each pigeon could fly with a dozen of them. In that way one of the birds could carry over 30,000 messages at one time.

When the pigeons arrived in Paris, the tiny rolls of film with all the letters printed on them were flattened out, and with a magic lantern were shown in larger size on a screen. The many letters were then copied by clerks and were sent on to the right people.

It was a very profitable postal business. Since the French government charged ten cents a word for letters carried by pigeon post, each little bird carried nearly fifty thousand dollars' worth of mail. A very valuable little pigeon, indeed!

## Airmail Balloon Post

The balloons carrying the mail out of Paris became a regular postal service during the war. Manned by French postmen, the large balloons carried mail to other parts of France and to England, in spite of the German gunners who tried to shoot them down.

The French balloon postmen carried millions of letters across the German lines during the days and nights of that war. Some of the men lost their lives doing their duty carrying the mail through. Other French postmen died heroic deaths as they tried again and again to get mail in and out of Paris. As they went through the German lines some postmen tried to disguise themselves and fool the German soldiers, but sometimes they were caught.

## Airmail, Airplanes, and Jets

On September 24, 1911, eight years after the first successful flight of an airplane in America, mail carried by an airplane was flown from Garden City, Long Island, to Mineola, Long Island, a distance of six miles. For the next few years the early airplanes flew the mail short distances in about sixteen states.

There were not many landing fields in the United States and not many air pilots who were willing to risk their lives carrying mail in those rickety early

planes in bad weather. But when the United States went to war against Germany in World War I, the airmail service became very busy.

As planes improved, the airmail service improved. In 1920, planes carrying mail flew across the whole United States. And now, in present days, very fast planes, jets carrying mail, fly across the oceans to every part of the world.

Now that all the people of the world can send messages to one another and begin to understand one another better, we hope that we all can become good neighbors.

# The U.S. Postal Service

The postal service of the United States does a great deal to help people all over the world, both in this country and in distant lands, to understand one another because they can exchange ideas through the mails. Over 500,000 people work in the United States postal service.

The postman whom you see delivering and gathering mail did not always wear a handsome blue-gray uniform. Over a hundred years ago our postmen wore ordinary clothes.

The U.S. Post Office records show that the mail carrier's uniform was first worn in Detroit, Michigan, in 1868. It was something like that worn by our modern postmen except that in those days a straw hat was worn in the summertime, and U.S. Army overcoats in the wintertime.

The railway mail clerks were put into uniform in 1877 by the postmaster general, but they wore uniforms for only two years. Then mail clerks on the trains were ordered to wear regular clothes with a special cap, a badge, and a gun to protect the mail from train robbers. Badges and guns must be worn by railway mail clerks in these days, too.

The modern United States postman has a summer uniform as well as a winter one. And there are some United States postal delivery men who wear snowshoes and fur parkas a great deal of the time. They are the postmen who carry the mail in Alaska, where summer is short.

There are also United States postmen who almost always wear just caps, light trousers, and light shirts. They are the postmen who carry the mail in the fiftieth state of the Union, Hawaii.

Thousands of postmen and postwomen wear no uniform. They are the postal clerks who work in the regular post offices and in the big main post offices, sorting out the mail as it is received and sending it out to be delivered by the uniformed postmen.

Women postal clerks as well as men sort and postmark the mail in the main post office after the mail trucks and the mail trains deliver it. All sorts of wonderful machines help the postal clerks sort

the mail. But every one of those letters, cards, or packages that make up the mountain of 200 million pieces of mail that daily go through the post must be looked at and the addresses must be read by a number of people who work in the post offices.

Each piece of that 200-million-piece pile must be handled and must receive personal attention.

This is what happens to the letter you mail, from the time you put it in the mailbox until it is delivered to your friend in Kokomo. Or does she live in Kalamazoo?

**1**
YOU MAIL THE LETTER
TO YOUR FRIEND.

**2**
YOUR LETTER AND A LOT OF OTHERS
ARE COLLECTED

**3**
AND RUSHED TO THE
POST OFFICE

**7**
...NOW BUNDLED AND TIED
OUT TO SPECIFIC PLACES,

**8**
PLACED IN        MAIL POUCHES

**9**
AND    DISPATCHED...

**12**
WHERE THEY ARE SORTED TO
PROPER STATION

SECONDARY

**13**
THEN RUSHED TO DELIVERY
STATION

**14**
...NOW SORTED TO PROPER
CARRIER ROUTE

PRIMARY

That is a lot of good work done for only five cents, the price of a stamp for a first class letter.

When a letter is properly stamped and properly addressed, the postal clerks can send it quickly on its way as soon as it is received in the main post office. If a letter received in the main post office is

10
TO TRUCKS, AIRPLANES, TRAINS OR    SHIPS

11
ON ARRIVAL AT DESTINATION
SPED TO POST OFFICE

15
THEN TO STREET ADDRESS

16
AT LAST YOUR LETTER IS CARRIED
BY THE POST MAN

17
AND DELIVERED RIGHT TO
YOUR FRIENDS
DOOR!

not properly addressed or stamped, things are not
so easy.

The postal clerks in the main post office have two
ways of handling a difficult letter. If the letter has
been sent without a proper address from some-
where in the United States, that letter is returned

to the person who sent it — if there is a return address on the envelope.

But if such a letter has been sent from a foreign land, that letter is treated in another way. The letter is passed on to the "Hards" section of the main post office. The postal clerks in the "Hards" section study the address on the envelope. It may have been written by a foreign person who could not write English very well or was unfamiliar with the way addresses are written in the United States.

For example, an envelope addressed like this,

may be corrected this way.

Since there is no 369th Street in New York City, that was an easy one to correct.

But sometimes the addresses are really hard to read. That is why they go to what is called the "Hards" section.

For example,

Perhaps that letter should have been addressed like this.

The postal clerks who work in the "Hards" section are alert. But that is true of all the people who work in the postal service. Everyone must be able to read quickly and to figure things out.

If a letter or a package does not carry enough stamps, it is either returned to the sender, or the postman tries to collect the postal money from the receiver.

There are a number of other special departments in the postal service. One of them is called the Department of Postal Inspection. The postal inspectors watch out for suspicious-looking letters and packages that are sent through the mails. If necessary, they open and examine them.

Sometimes packages carrying explosives and bombs are sent by nasty or mentally sick people or by spies. The postal inspectors also watch out for packages that may be sent by smugglers trying to get valuable things into the country without paying the import tax they ought to pay. And the inspectors watch out for thieves who try to send their loot through the mail.

Of course, the inspectors do not tamper with any mail unless they have a very good reason. If they do open an innocent letter or package by mistake, they write a note on the envelope and explain their mistake.

# Unclaimed and Damaged Merchandise

If a package cannot be delivered because it has a wrong address and there is no return address on the package, or if the people to whom it is addressed will not accept the package because it has been damaged, or if for some reason it is unclaimed, the main post office stores that package.

Then, twice a year, during the month of June and again every October, the post office has a big auction sale. All the things that had been stored from those packages are auctioned off. Such goods as collapsible rowboats, secondhand automobile tires, cameras, books, and even precious jewels are among the many things that have been sold.

The day before the auction, people are allowed to look at the things that are to be sold. Sometimes, in the goods up for auction, people find something from a package that they had mailed. The package must have lost its address in some way. That is why it is there.

There is very little reason why anyone's package should land in the Unclaimed and Damaged Merchandise Department. Wrap your package well, write clearly on the wrapping the proper address and your own return address, including the zip code numbers for both, put the proper stamp on the package, and it should go through the mail. In the post office the postal clerk will tell you how much the stamps for the package will cost and

what the proper zip code numbers are, if you do not know them. It is very important to put the zip code numbers on the address. Your package will travel faster if they are there.

Do you know how many classes of mail there are? Well, there is first class mail, for letters or very important small packages. That is the most expensive class. A first class letter sent special delivery by airmail is the quickest way you can get your letters delivered. You can send packages that way, too. Remember, though, it is expensive.

There are also second class, third class, and fourth class mail. Fourth class is the cheapest way to send anything through the mail. Parcels, books, and catalogs are usually sent by fourth class mail.

You can send money through the mail safely by getting a money order at the post office. And you can insure a letter or a package so that it will get special attention all the time it is traveling from one place to another.

If you do not know exactly how to send something through the mail, or how much it will cost, ask the postal clerk in your post office. He will be glad to help you.

# You, A Postman?

And now that we have come to the end of this book, here is a question. Would you like to be a postman or work as a postal clerk in the post office?

You cannot just walk in and ask for a job. Here is what you must do.

You must take an examination — a civil service examination. Almost everyone who works for the United States government must take a civil service examination, except the people who are elected at the polls, or who are appointed by someone already in office.

If you pass your examination with a high rating and if you can prove you are a good citizen, you may get a job in the United States postal service.

The head of the whole postal service is the postmaster general. He is appointed by the President of the United States. He is also a member of the President's Cabinet and is usually a good businessman (or possibly a businesswoman) who knows how to run an organization as big and as important as the United States postal service.

The postmasters all over the country are appointed, whether the post office is in a big city like New York, which handles over 20 million pieces of mail a day and employs 34,000 men and women, or in a sleepy little village.

Do you know that the postmen who carry the mail to the houses in your town do that because they want to? It is true. When they take their examination for the job in the post office they write down whether they want to work in the post office as a postal clerk or whether they want to be a postman who delivers and gathers the mail outside the post office.

So make up your mind. Do you want to be a postman in a handsome blue-gray uniform, or do you want to do the many interesting things that the postal clerks do indoors?

In either case you will be working with fine, bright, honest people who know how to read quickly and how to figure things out.

And you too will become a person who helps people all over this country and all over the world to understand one another better because they can send written messages back and forth. As a postman you will help all the world's people to become good friends and neighbors.

# Index